Trace & Learn
UNICORN
Handwriting Practice

Text: Elizabeth Golding
Illustrations: Lisa Mallett
Design: Anton Poitier

iseek

My name is

I like

unicorns

Printed in China.

Help your child develop handwriting skills

Use this book to encourage your child to learn the letters of the alphabet and practice their handwriting skills, using both UPPERCASE and lowercase letters. This book is typeset in Sassoon, a typeface developed by Rosemary Sassoon after researching what letterforms children found easiest to read. This typeface is widely used in schools to teach reading and handwriting.

Here are the main handwriting styles that are typically taught:
Print: The letters do not join and have various start and finish points for each letter.
Cursive: The letters have starting points in print, but exit strokes, or tails, are also included.
Continuous cursive: The letters are joined together in a continuous flow of connected writing.

In Sassoon lowercase letterforms, the exit strokes link together visually, making an understandable link from print to continuous cursive writing.

This book uses a unicorn theme to motivate early readers. There are lots of pictures, which you can use to encourage your child to color after tracing and copying the letters.

A is for Apple

a is in hat

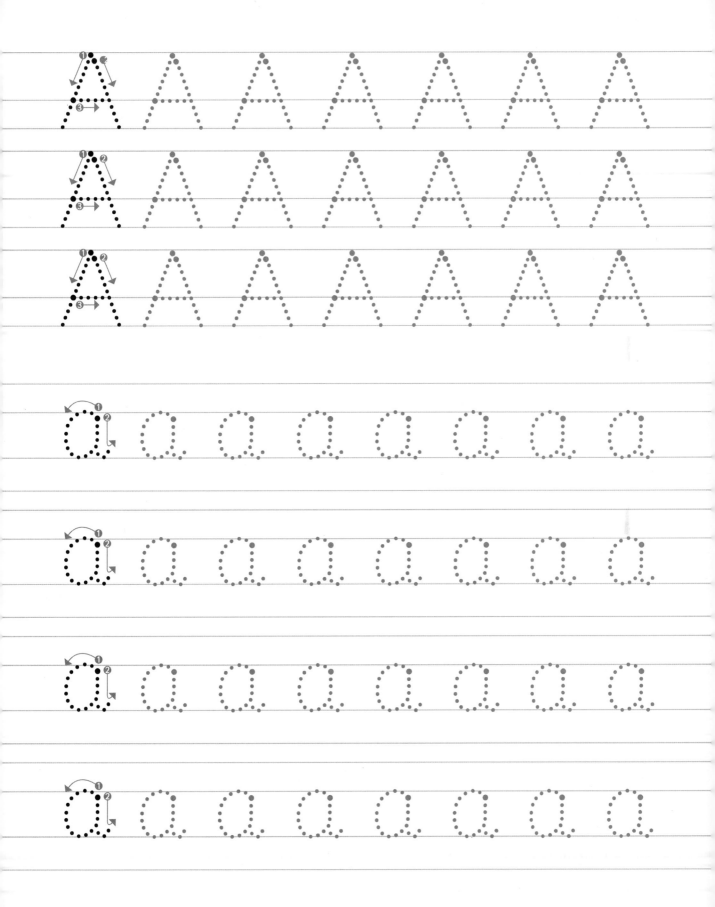

B is for Butterfly

b is in crab

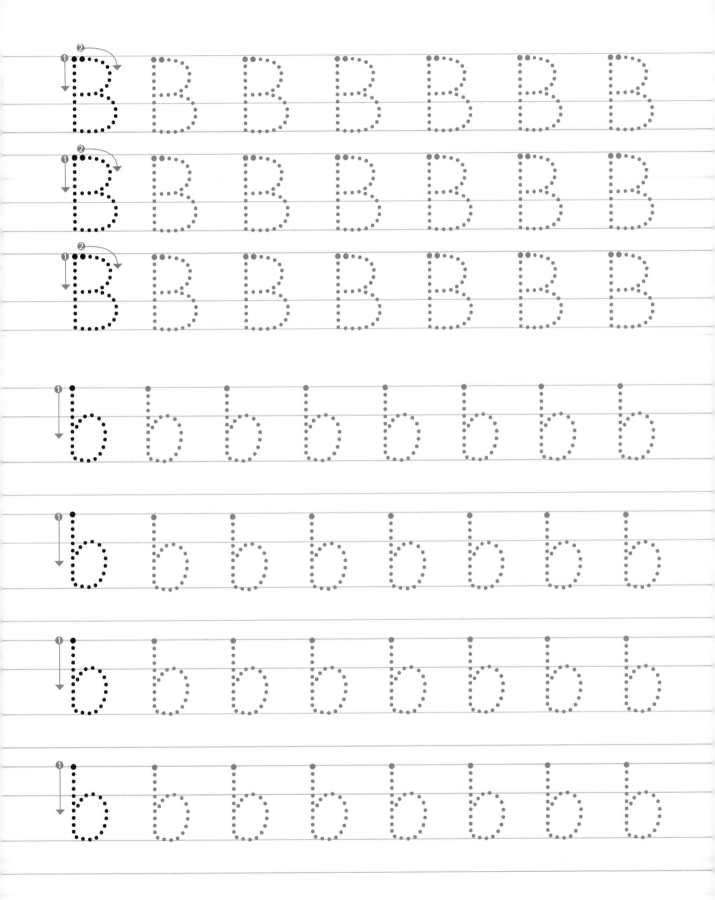

C is for Ċat

c is in cloċk

D is for Dragon

d is in gold

E is for Elf

e is in hen

E E E E E E E E

E E E E E E E E

E E E E E E E E

e e e e e e e e e

e e e e e e e e e

e e e e e e e e e

e e e e e e e e e

F is for Fairy

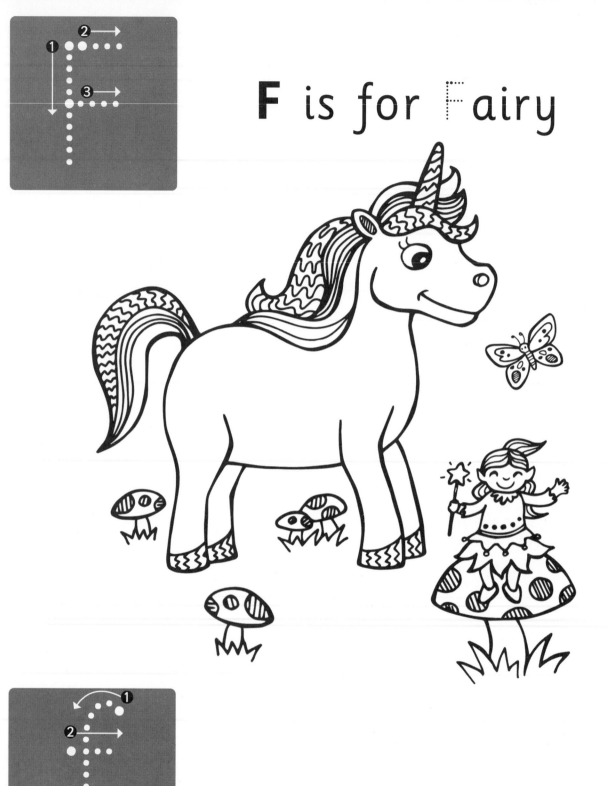

f is in butterfly

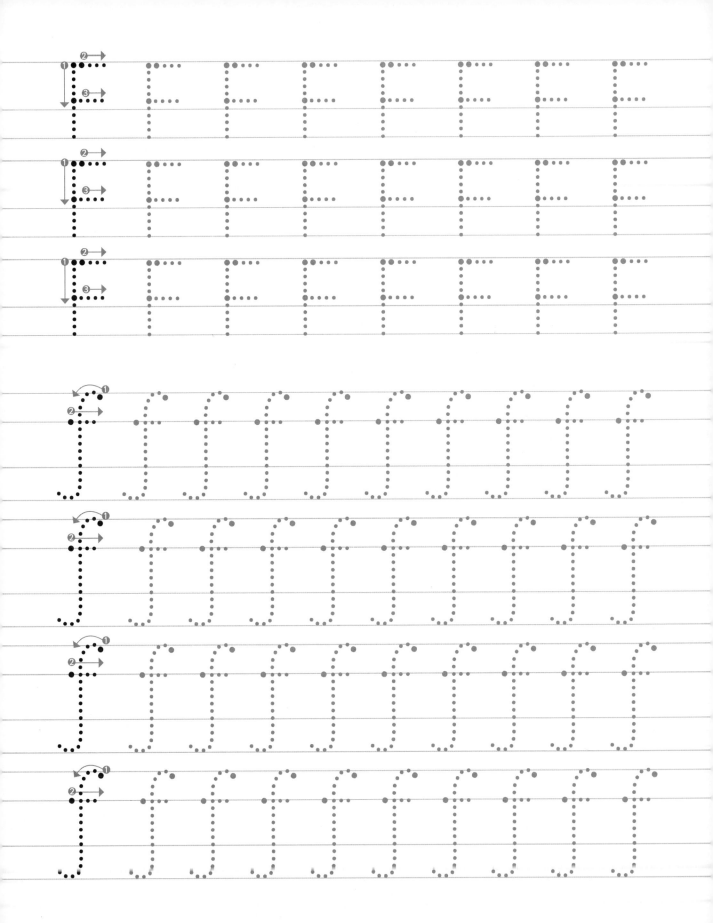

G is for Giant

g is in frog

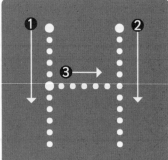

H is for Hat

h is in chair

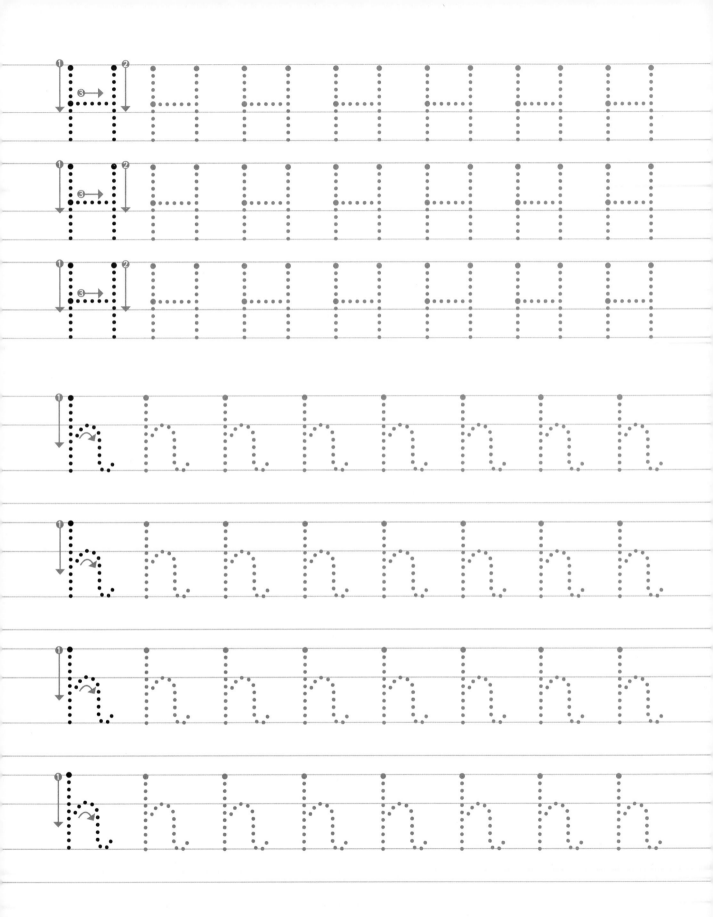

I is for Ink

i is in giant

I I I I I I I I I

I I I I I I I I I

I I I I I I I I I

l l l l l l l l l l

l l l l l l l l l l

l l l l l l l l l l

l l l l l l l l l l

J is for Jester

j is in pajamas

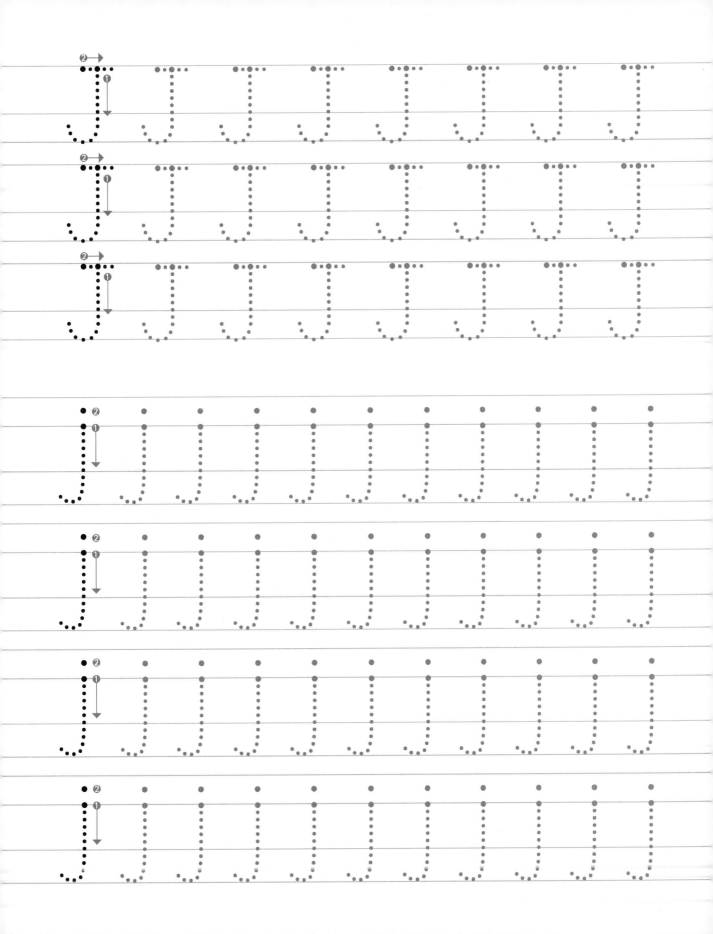

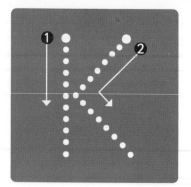

K is for King

k is in cake

L is for Lion

l is in girl

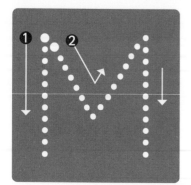

M is for Monster

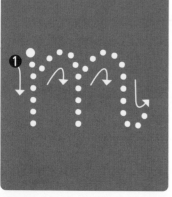

m is in mermaid

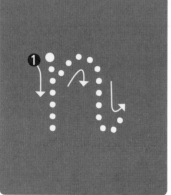

N is for Nest

n is in sun

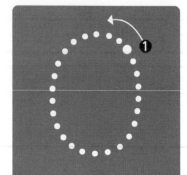

O is for ○gre

o is in s○cks

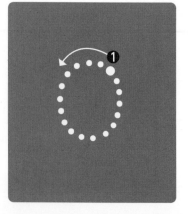

P is for Prince

p is in slippers

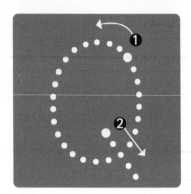

Q is for Queen

q is in squirrel

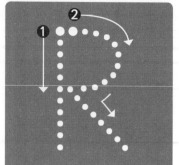

R is for Rapunzel

r is in forest

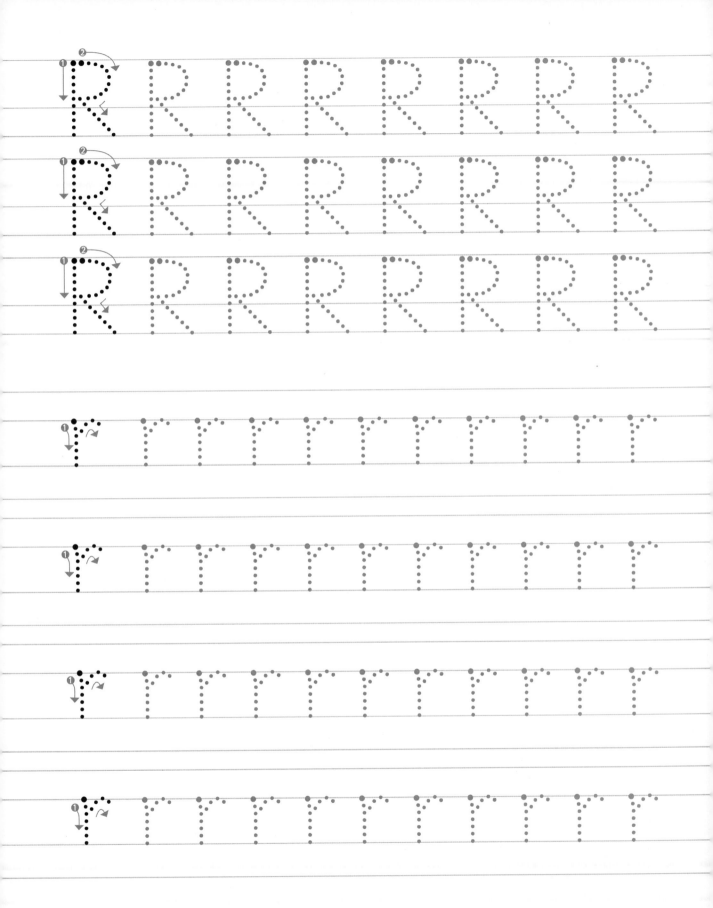

S is for Spells

s is in flowers

S S S S S S S S

S S S S S S S S

S S S S S S S S

S S S S S S S S S S

S S S S S S S S S S

S S S S S S S S S S

S S S S S S S S S S

T is for Tiara

t is in witch

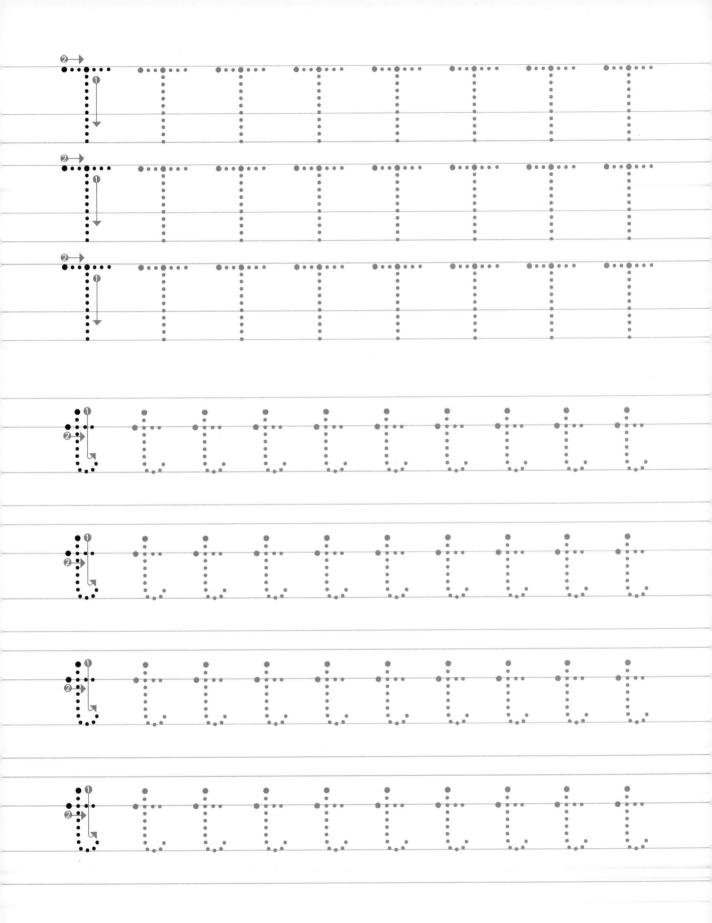

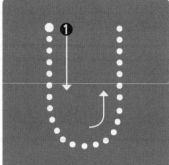

U is for Unicorn

u is in cup

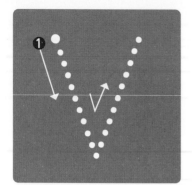

V is for Volcano

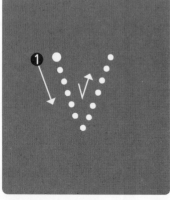

v is in dove

V V V V V V V V V V

V V V V V V V V V V

V V V V V V V V V V

v v v v v v v v v v

v v v v v v v v v v

v v v v v v v v v v

v v v v v v v v v v

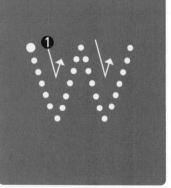

W is for Wand

w is in tower

W W W W W W W W

W W W W W W W W

W W W W W W W W

w w w w w w w w

w w w w w w w w

w w w w w w w w

w w w w w w w w

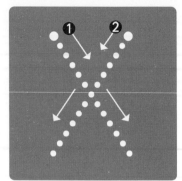

X is for X-ray

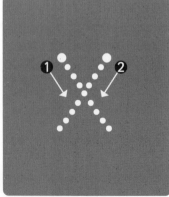

x is in box

Y is for Yo-yo

y is in boy

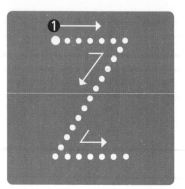

Z is for Zebra

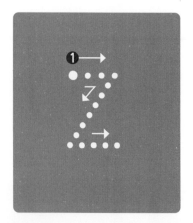

z is in maze

Practice the letter **A**

Practice the letter **B**

Practice the letter **C**

Practice the letter **D**

Practice the letter **E**

Ee Ee Ee Ee Ee

Ee Ee Ee Ee Ee

Ee Ee Ee Ee Ee

Ee Ee Ee Ee Ee

Ee Ee Ee Ee Ee

Ee Ee Ee Ee Ee

Practice the letter **F**

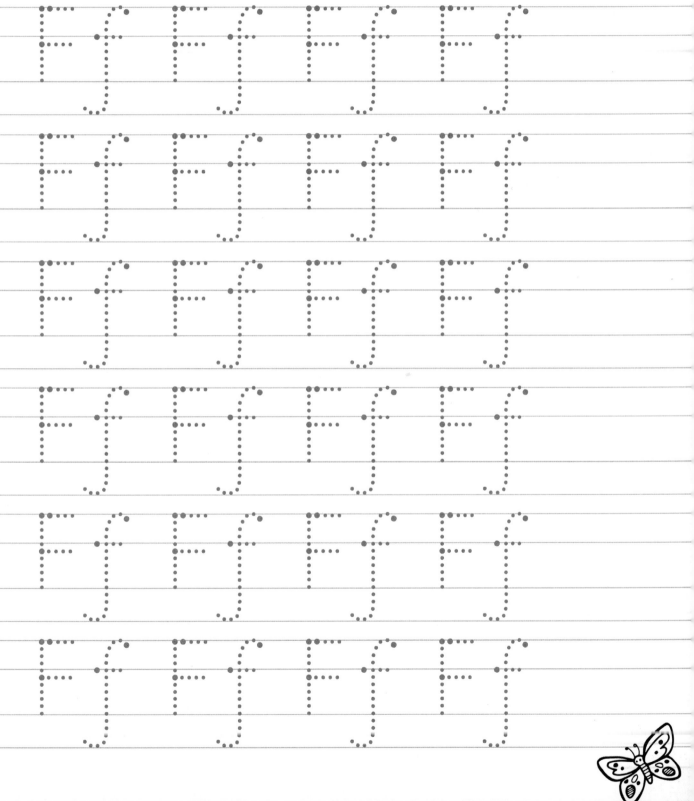

Practice the letter **G**

Practice the letter **H**

Practice the letter **I**

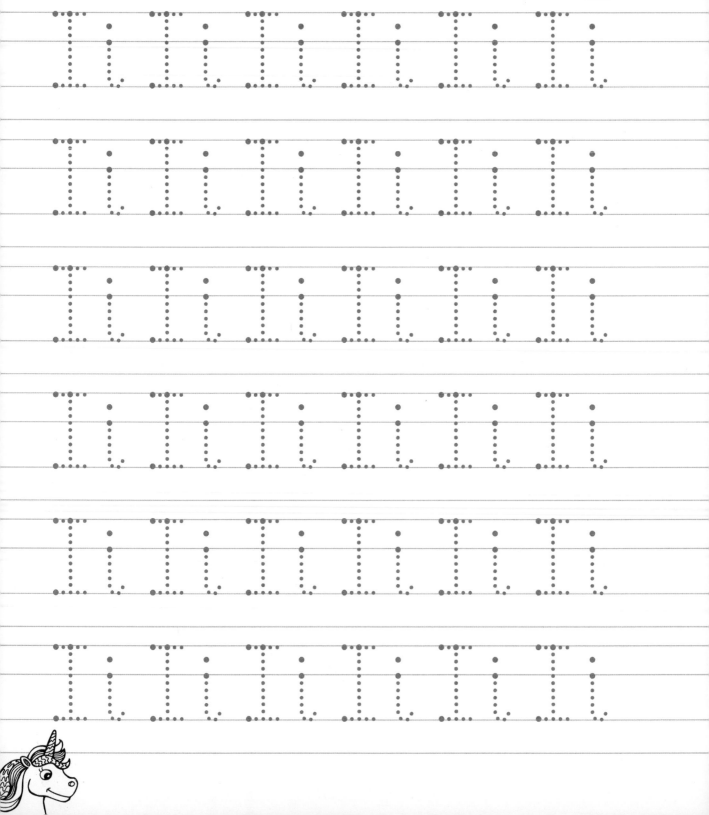

Practice the letter **J**

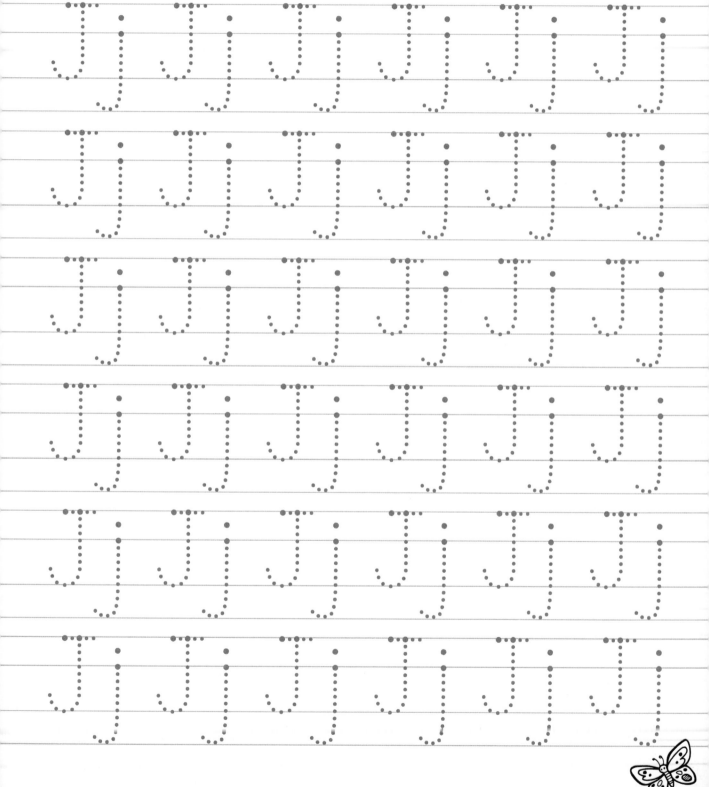

Practice the letter **K**

Practice the letter **L**

Practice the letter **M**

Mm Mm Mm

Mm Mm Mm

Mm Mm Mm

Mm Mm Mm

Mm Mm Mm

Mm Mm Mm

Practice the letter **N**

Nn Nn Nn Nn Nn

Nn Nn Nn Nn Nn

Nn Nn Nn Nn Nn

Nn Nn Nn Nn Nn

Nn Nn Nn Nn Nn

Nn Nn Nn Nn Nn

Practice the letter O

Practice the letter **P**

Practice the letter Q

Practice the letter **R**

Practice the letter **S**

Practice the letter **T**

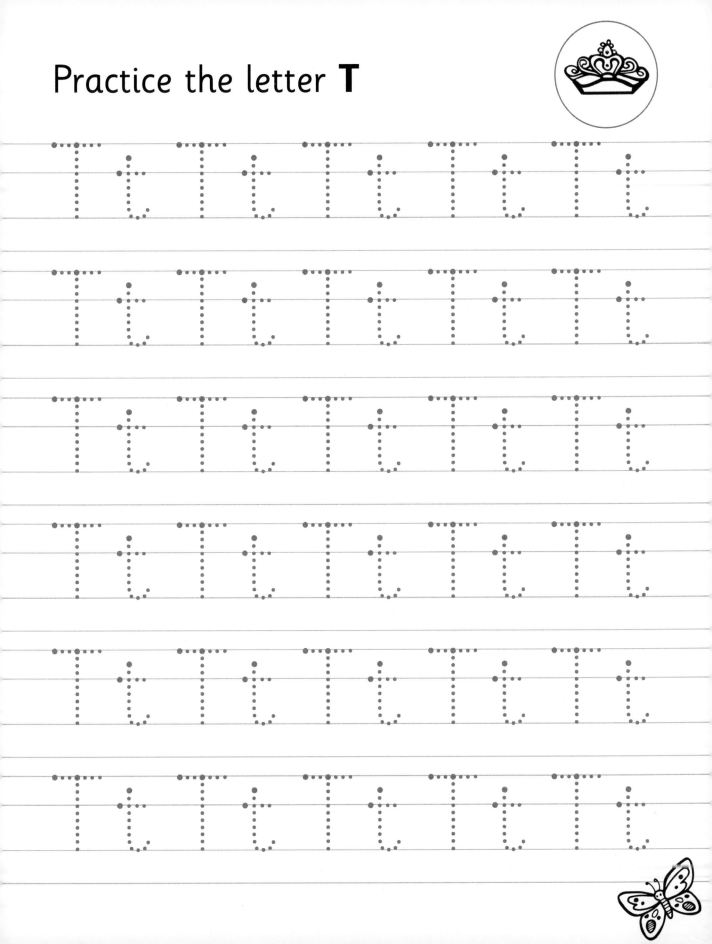

Tt Tt Tt Tt Tt Tt

Tt Tt Tt Tt Tt

Tt Tt Tt Tt Tt

Tt Tt Tt Tt Tt

Tt Tt Tt Tt Tt

Tt Tt Tt Tt Tt

Practice the letter U

Uu Uu Uu Uu Uu

Uu Uu Uu Uu Uu

Uu Uu Uu Uu Uu

Uu Uu Uu Uu Uu

Uu Uu Uu Uu Uu

Uu Uu Uu Uu Uu

Practice the letter **V**

Practice the letter W

W w W w W w
W w W w W w
W w W w W w
W w W w W w
W w W w W w
W w W w W w

Practice the letter X

Practice the letter Y

Practice the letter Z

Copy the fairy-tale words

Star

Star

Star

Star

Star

Star

Unicorn

Unicorn

Unicorn

Unicorn

Unicorn

Unicorn

Copy the fairy-tale word

Fairy

Fairy

Copy the fairy-tale word

Princess

Princess

Copy the fairy-tale word

Rainbow

Rainbow

Copy the fairy-tale word

ice cream

ice cream

Copy the fairy-tale word

Umbrella

Umbrella

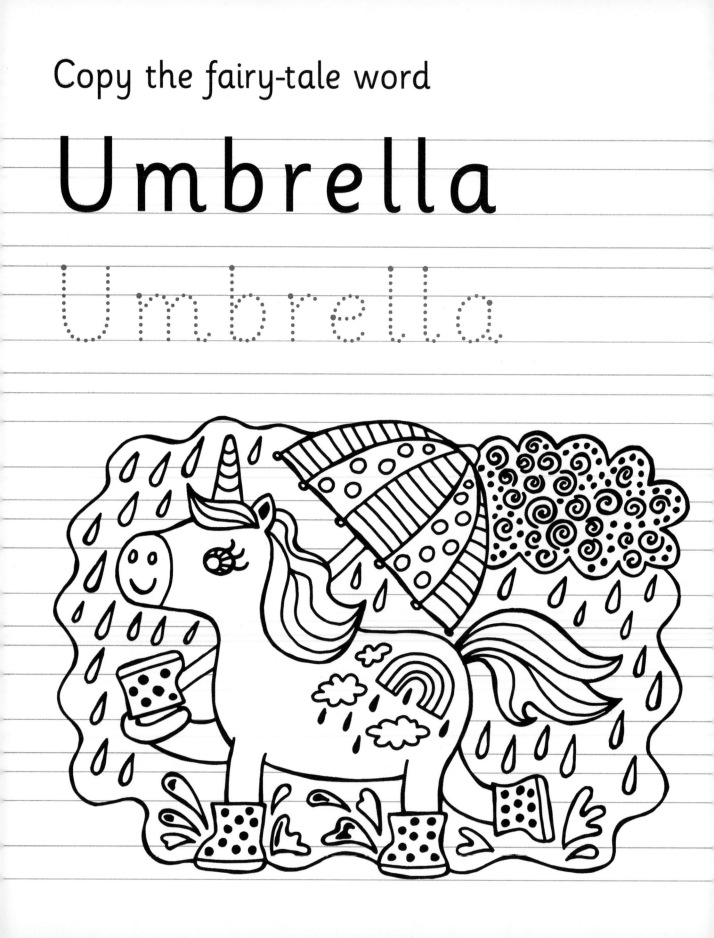

Copy the fairy-tale word

Heart

Heart

Write the alphabet

a b c d e f g h i

j k l m n o p q r

s t u v w x y z

A B C D E F G H I

J K L M N O P Q R

S T U V W X Y Z